# Facts About the Jellyfish

## By Lisa Strattin

## © 2019 Lisa Strattin

D1707376

# FREE BOOK

## FREE FOR ALL SUBSCRIBERS

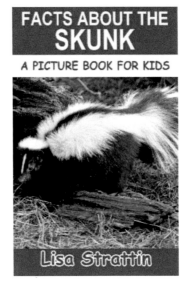

LisaStrattin.com/Subscribe-Here

To Whom It May Concern:

I/We, _____ Theresa (Tracy) Kadonaga and Tetsuo (Tex) Kadonaga _____

(Full Name(s) of Custodial and/or Non-Custodial Parent(s)/Legal Guardian(s))

am/are the lawful custodial parent and/or non-custodial parent(s) or legal guardian(s) of:

Child's full name: _____ Mollyrose Miyo Kadonaga _____

Date of Birth: _____ May 2nd, 2013 _____

Place of Birth: _____ Upland, CA _____

U.S. Passport Number: _____ 641919523 _____

Date and Place of Issuance of U.S. Passport: _____ June 11, 2019 _____ California, United States

_____ Mollyrose Miyo Kadonaga _____,(Child's Full Name) has my/our consent to travel with:

Full name of accompanying person: _____ Tetsuo (Tex) Kadonaga _____

U.S. or foreign passport number: _____ Canadian Passport # HM415333 _____

Date and Place of issuance of this passport: _____ July 18, 2016 _____ Gatineau, Canada

Cambridge, Ontario CANADA _____ during the period of _____ August 1-14, 2022

To Whom It May Concern:

I/We, Theresa (Tracy) Kadonaga and Tetsuo (Tex) Kadonaga

(Full Name(s) of Custodial and/or Non-Custodial Parent(s)/Legal Guardian(s))

am/are the lawful custodial parent and/or non-custodial parent(s) or legal guardian(s) of:

Child's full name: Finnegan Kenji Kadonaga

Date of Birth: July 2nd, 2015

Place of Birth: Upland, CA

U.S. Passport Number: 641919523

Date and Place of Issuance of U.S. Passport: June 11, 2019 California, United States

Finnegan Kenji Kadonaga (Child's Full Name) has my/our consent to travel with:

Full name of accompanying person: Tetsuo (Tex) Kadonaga

U.S. or foreign passport number: Canadian Passport # HM415333

Date and Place of issuance of this passport: July 18, 2016 Gatineau, Canada

August 1-14, 2022

During that period, Finnegan Kenji Kadonaga (Child's Name) will be residing with

Miye & Paul Cox (Aunt & Uncle) at the following address:

Number/street address and apartment number: 40 Forestview Drive

City, State/Province, Country: Cambridge, Ontario, CANADA

Telephone and fax numbers (work, cell phone and residence) (w) 519-653-1111 (c) 519-212-0468 (h) 226-218-7328

**Parent(s) or Legal Guardian(s):**

Full Name: Tetsuo (Tex) Kadonaga

Signature: _____

Date: _____

Full Name: Theresa (Tracy) Kadonaga

Signature: _____

Date: _____

**Witnesses:**

Signed before me, _____,

this _____ (Date)

at _____. (Name of Location)

Signed before me, _____,

this _____ (Date)

at _____. (Name of Location)

Miye & Paul Cox (Aunt & Uncle) _____ at the following address:

Number/street address and apartment number: _____ 40 Forestview Drive _____

City, State/Province, Country: _____ Cambridge, Ontario, CANADA _____

Telephone and fax numbers (work, cell phone and residence) _____ (w) 519-653-1111 (c) 519-212-0468 (h) 226-218-7328

**Parent(s) or Legal Guardian(s):**

Full Name: _____ Tetsuo (Tex) Kadonaga _____

Signature: _____

Date: _____

Full Name: _____ Theresa (Tracy) Kadonaga _____

Signature: _____

Date: _____

**Witnesses:**

Signed before me, _____

this _____ (Date)

at _____ . (Name of Location)

Signed before me, _____

this _____ (Date)

at _____ . (Name of Location)

# BOX SET

- **FACTS ABOUT THE POISON DART FROGS**
- **FACTS ABOUT THE THREE TOED SLOTH**
  - **FACTS ABOUT THE RED PANDA**
  - **FACTS ABOUT THE SEAHORSE**
  - **FACTS ABOUT THE PLATYPUS**
  - **FACTS ABOUT THE REINDEER**
  - **FACTS ABOUT THE PANTHER**
- **FACTS ABOUT THE SIBERIAN HUSKY**

## LisaStrattin.com/BookBundle

Facts for Kids Picture Books by Lisa Strattin

Little Blue Penguin, Vol 92

Chipmunk, Vol 5

Frilled Lizard, Vol 39

Blue and Gold Macaw, Vol 13

Poison Dart Frogs, Vol 50

Blue Tarantula, Vol 115

African Elephants, Vol 8

Amur Leopard, Vol 89

Sabre Tooth Tiger, Vol 167

Baboon, Vol 174

Sign Up for New Release Emails Here

LisaStrattin.com/subscribe-here

Contents

# INTRODUCTION

Jellyfish, also known as jellies and sea jellies, are boneless animals are found floating freely through the oceans all around the world. They are particularly prominent in coastal areas, so if you visit the coast and go swimming in the ocean, you might see one.

## CHARACTERISTICS

There are thought to be around 2,000 different species of jellyfish, with the most common the big, colorful ones that are seen in warmer coastal areas. There are four different types of jellyfish that can be determined by their shape and the way they behave.

Some jellyfish stings contain poison which the is used to stun and kill prey. The box jellyfish, which is found in the oceans around Australia, has a sting powerful enough to be fatal to humans.

The long tentacles of the jellyfish are what produces the sting. It's been tried and tested - you can touch the top of the jellyfish without being hurt. But if you touch anywhere else, look out!

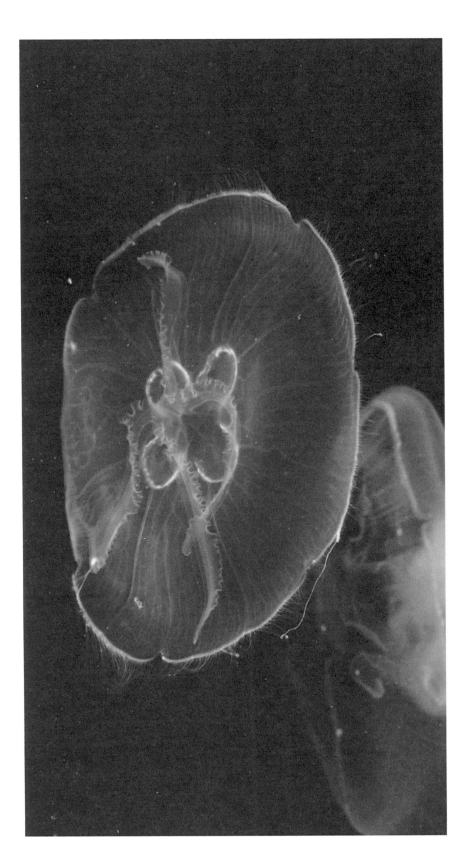

# APPEARANCE

Despite the name, jellyfish are not actually fish; they are classed in a group all their own because they are unlike any other animal on Earth. The body is made up of a non-living jelly-like substance called mesoglea. This is surrounded by a layer of skin that is just one cell thick. The body of the jellyfish is made up of 90% water.

Jellyfish also have tentacles around their mouths that vary in length depending on the species of jellyfish. The jellyfish use their tentacles to catch and sting their prey.

The tentacles of the jellyfish are covered in a skin that contains special cells, some that sting, some that grip and some that stick. The jellyfish is able to produce these cells at an alarming rate so they are effectively disposable to the jellyfish.

## LIFE STAGES

Jellyfish release their eggs and sperm into the water which eventually meet and the egg is fertilized. The jellyfish egg quickly becomes an embryo and begins to develop in its water world. A jellyfish is on its own from the beginning!

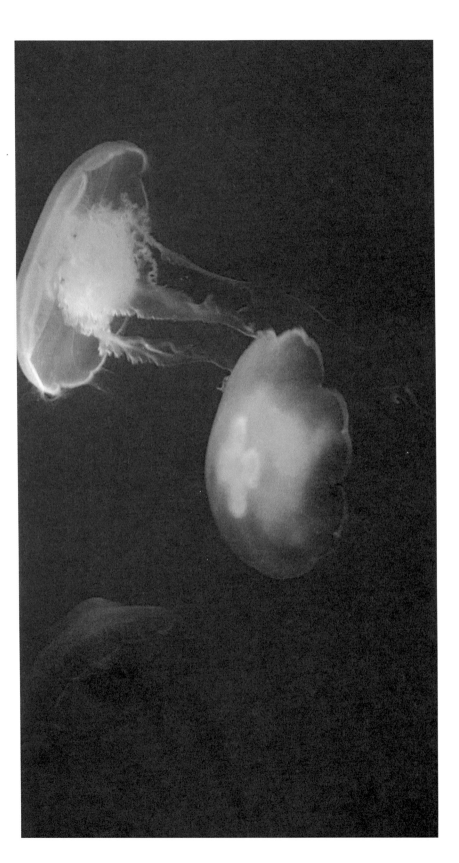

## LIFE SPAN

Jellyfish live from 1-5 years, depending on the species and whether or not it is able to avoid predators in the water where it lives.

## SIZE

Jellyfish can be found in all shapes and sizes from just a few inches in diameter to over 3 feet long. Although, as of this writing in 2019, there was discovery of jellyfish in the ocean that was taller than a man!

## HABITAT

Jellyfish live in the ocean – all oceans, all around the world. You have a good chance of seeing some of them in coastal waters if you swim there.

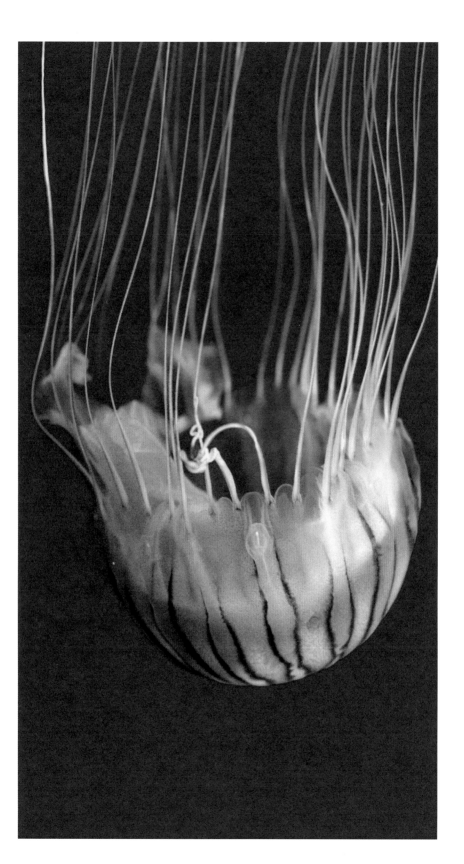

## DIET

The jellyfish is a carnivorous animal is a very efficient predator. They use their tentacles to stun prey before grabbing onto it and bringing it into their mouth to eat. They prey on all kinds of aquatic animals such as small fish, eggs and invertebrates along with anything else that gets stuck in their tentacles.

## ENEMIES

Because many species of jellyfish are transparent, they are often hard for predators to spot. However, they are slow-moving, drifting through the water. Sometimes they use their tentacles to propel them along.

Jellyfish are eaten by humans, sharks, squid and occasionally birds.

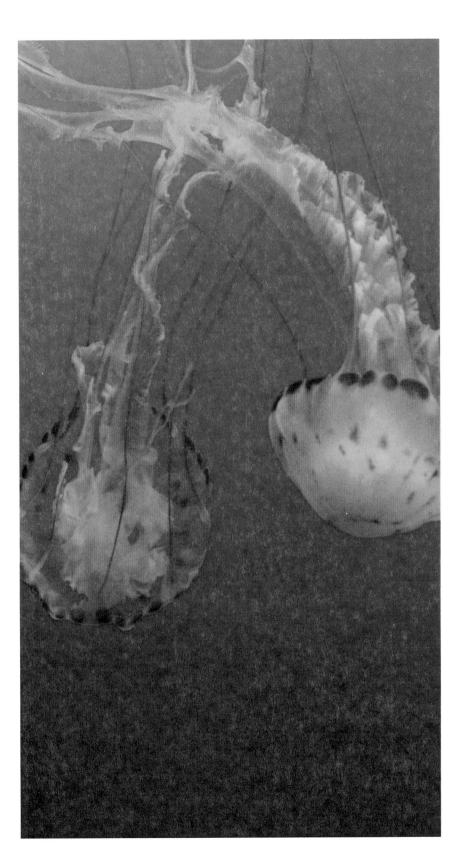

## SUITABILITY AS PETS

Jellyfish, at least some species, can be kept as pets. You will need a special tank that has rounded corners because they can get trapped and stuck in a rectangular tank. You can certainly learn more about them from a marine animal pet store if you want to keep one!

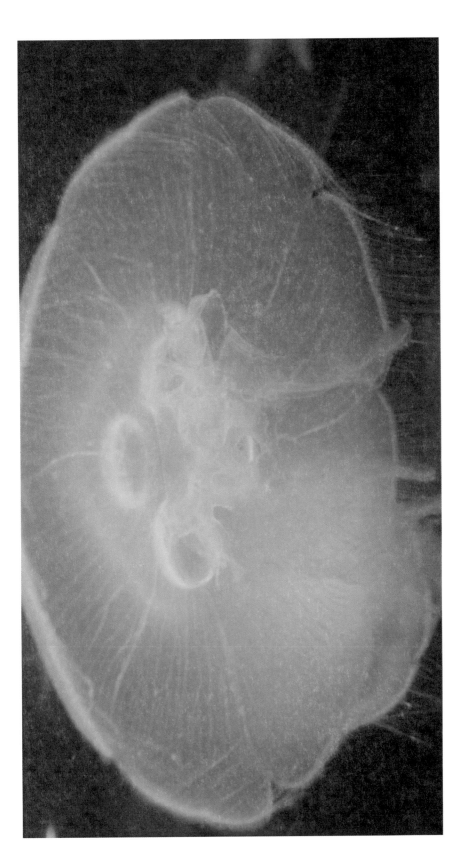

# COLOR ME

# COLOR ME

# COLOR ME

# COLOR ME

# COLOR ME

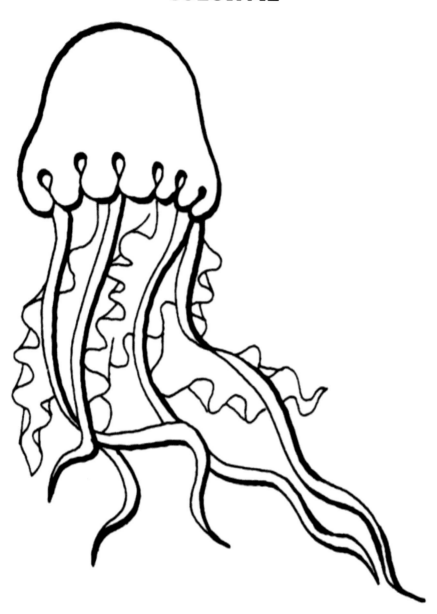

# COLOR ME

# COLOR ME

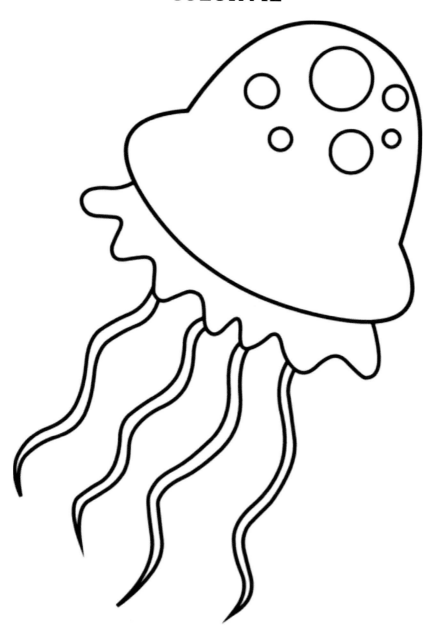

# COLOR ME

# COLOR ME

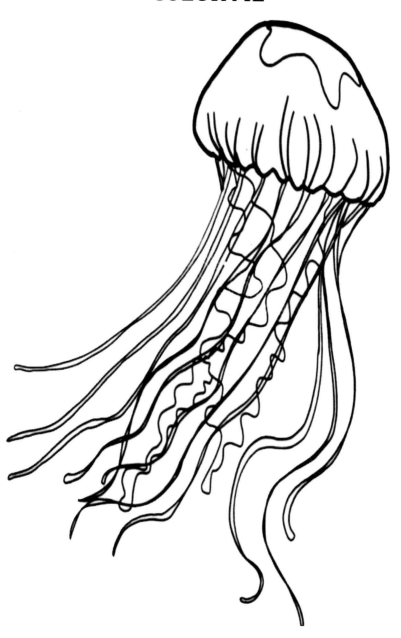

# COLOR ME

Please leave me a review here:

*LisaStrattin.com/Review-Vol-206*

For more Kindle Downloads Visit Lisa Strattin
Author Page on Amazon Author Central

*amazon.com/author/lisastrattin*

To see upcoming titles, visit my website at
LisaStrattin.com– most books available on Kindle!

*LisaStrattin.com*

# FREE BOOK

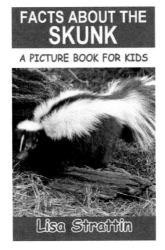

Made in the USA
Las Vegas, NV
25 May 2022

49358810R00026